LIFE SKILLS

Public Speaking

HERON
BOOKS
K-12 CURRICULUM

At Heron Books, we think learning should be engaging and fun. It should be hands-on and it should allow students to move at their own pace.

For this purpose, we have created an accompanying learning guide to help the student progress through this book, chapter by chapter, with increasing confidence, interest and independence.

Get your free learning guide at
heronbooks.com/learningguides.

For a final exam, email
teacherresources@heronbooks.com.

We would love to hear from you!
Email us at *feedback@heronbooks.com.*

Published by
Heron Books, Inc.
20950 SW Rock Creek Road
Sheridan, OR 97378

heronbooks.com

———————

Special thanks to all the teachers and students who provided feedback instrumental to this edition.

———————

CONTENTS

1

Public Speaking Introduction

Public Speaking Introduction

1

PUBLIC SPEAKING? WHO, ME?

For many people the thought of speaking in public makes them a little nervous. For some, the thought of it makes them *very* nervous. For a few, the thought of it is, frankly, terrifying. On the other hand, some people find public speaking easy and enjoyable.

Like anything else, public speaking can be studied and learned and, with practice, anyone can become an effective public speaker. And if you have ever watched someone giving an effective public presentation and thought, "Wow, this person is such a great speaker, so relaxed, so natural," you might be surprised to discover that quite often such speakers aren't really as "relaxed" and "natural" as they appear. But they may be well-practiced, and as part of that they've learned to look relaxed and natural!

As with any other skill, practice is key.

THE FOCUS OF THE COURSE

Thus, though there will be some things to study, read, research and learn, the emphasis of the course and the majority of time spent will be on

PRACTICE.

In fact, by the end of this course, you will have done at least two dozen speeches.

SOME OTHER THINGS TO KNOW

- Because the emphasis is on practice and the intent is to have you spend as much time as possible actually giving talks, the course will not emphasize researching topics for speeches. It is encouraged that you make use of research already done from other studies, and that you generally choose topics you are already very familiar with.

- It is also advised that you look over the learning guide to see what types of talks you will be expected to do. Make some notes on what topics you think might work best at the different points throughout the course.

- As an aid to your study of public speaking, you will be video recording every talk you do. The quality of the videos will not be important as long as the image and sound are clear enough to be understood. Be sure you are prepared to store them until the course is done. You are not required to watch every speech you video, but they should always be available for review.

- The course is designed to be done with a study partner. You and your study partner will form an important team in assisting each other. If problems or disagreements come up, get them resolved quickly. The quality of the assistance you and your study partner provide each other will probably have a greater impact on the speed and effectiveness of the course than any other single factor.

- You will find the words "speeches," "talks" and "presentations" used throughout the course with generally the same intended meaning: an organized, intentional communication to a small or large group in a public or semi-public setting. If you want to sound more formal, call it a "speech." Less formal, a "talk." More informative, a "presentation." For the most part, there's no differentiation intended in the use of these terms in this course.

THE PLAN—EIGHT EASY STEPS

Here's the simple outline of the course:

1. ESTABLISHING THE FLIGHT PLAN

   That's what we're doing right now with this introduction to the course.

2. STARTING THE ENGINE

   How will we get the engine started? Have you give a speech! And not just any speech, but one on the subject of public speaking. That's right—before you study anything about public speaking, you will give a speech on public speaking. But don't worry. It will just be to your study partner and it's just to get you warmed up to the subject.

3. GETTING OFF THE GROUND

   Next you will look at what you already know that relates to effective communication and speaking. You may find you already know a lot more than you realized. After looking this over in some detail, you will prepare and give another talk, this time to gradually increasing numbers until you feel comfortable speaking in front of eight people. In this way, you will be introduced to public speaking smoothly and easily.

4. TAKING FLIGHT

   This will cover the most common types of speeches as well as some basics on writing and delivering speeches. And, of course, more practice.

5. LIFT-OFFS, LANDINGS AND COMMON PRECAUTIONS

   This section will give you a chance to look more closely at ways talks can be most effectively started and ended. It will also cover some common errors made in public speaking. By this time, you will be well along in developing your "successful talk checklist." This is your own list of public speaking do's and don'ts based on what you are learning as you do more and more talks. In this section, you will be able to work on any weak areas in your public speaking as needed. And, yes, this section will include giving more talks!

6. FLIGHT TIPS FROM PROFESSIONALS

Here you will get to spend a little time researching public speaking advice and tips from experienced speakers, garnering things you may want to add to your successful talk checklist.

7. TAKING SOME TRIPS

Yes, that's right—more practice, more speeches!

8. GETTING YOUR WINGS[1]

This is the final section of the course. You will give a major talk that must be passed by your academic supervisor. You will then end the course the way you began—with a short talk on the subject of public speaking. By this point you should feel confident of having achieved the course purpose: *Gain the skill to communicate effectively in public settings.*

Ready to start the engine?

---

1 **Earn (or get) one's wings:** prove oneself competent at something; officially become a pilot. From the wing-shaped insignia awarded to graduating pilots and often worn on a pilot's uniform.

2

What You Already Know About Public Speaking

What You Already Know About Public Speaking 2

What makes up a successful public presentation? For the sake of discussion, let's start with the following broad categories of things to consider:

A. The Venue Set-up

B. The Written Talk

C. The Presentation

Let's break these first two down a bit.

A. The Venue Set-up

- Neat, clean, orderly, reserved for the presentation
- Comfortable temperature, adequate ventilation
- Adequate, comfortable seating for attendees
- Adequate lighting
- Any sound system adequate, set up, tested and functioning properly
- Any audio-visual system and equipment operational and ready to go
- A dais, podium or suitable place for the speaker to talk from
- Coffee, tea, water available for attendees, if appropriate

This is just a quick list. There could be other things to consider as part of ensuring the venue is adequately set up.

B. The Written Talk

- Well researched (as appropriate)

- Logical

- Effectively organized to achieve its communication result

- Free of errors, appropriate and respectful of the audience and others

- Adequately interesting with audio-visual aids as useful

- Not too long or too short for purpose and context

- Understandable/suitable to target audience

- Honest and true, not plagiarized or otherwise phony

Again, that's a start. You might make the list differently or add other things to this list.

Note that so far we have a list of 16 things to think about to help keep a public speech from failing and we haven't even gotten to the actual speech yet!

One might consider all the above "common sense" points, but they aren't common sense to you if you've never thought about them or learned them from experience. One might also consider these categories "someone else's job," particularly the first. However, successful speakers never assume anything, including the fact that their speechwriter (when they have one) has written something that will work.

WHAT YOU ALREADY KNOW

In thinking about public speaking and what you are hoping to learn about it, the third category, the presentation itself, is the one you've probably been thinking about.

Well, it's possible that this is the category you already know the most about without even realizing it.

If you know anything about communication, you know something about public speaking, because public speaking is nothing if not communication. There are basics such as actually looking others in the eye, communicating clearly, listening well, letting others know you see and respect them—these sorts of basic communication skills translate directly over to public speaking.

If you know anything about the subject of study skills and what prevents or barriers successful learning, then you probably know some things to avoid or how to prevent a talk from putting your audience to sleep or leaving them bored.

Beyond these fundamental skills, there may be other skills you already have that could come into play in giving a public presentation. If you have any experience in acting, comedy, debate or other types of presentation or performance, even competitive sports, you may have skills you didn't realize often translate over into public speaking quite well. Even skills as an organizer, designer, visual artist, photographer, musician or filmmaker can play a role in how you design communication aids as simple as a digital slide presentation or as complex as a short film.

Let's go back for a moment to the second broad category, the written talk.

Notice that your skills in research, writing and logic, and your ability to put those together in a way that communicates honestly and effectively, are fundamental to effective public speaking—assuming, of course, you are writing your own talk.

The point here is simply this: Before launching into a study of the subject of public speaking, it's important for you to notice how much you already know.

Effectively using what you already know, you may find yourself well on your way to successful public speaking without adding much more than a little practice speaking in public!

3

Types of Speeches

Types of Speeches 3

It is usually considered that there are three main types of public speeches or presentations: *Informative*, *Persuasive*, and *Special Occasion.*

Let's take a brief look at each of these types.

INFORMATIVE

If you are informing your audience of something, you could call it an "informative speech." Here are some examples:

- Giving a lecture, a lesson or a presentation in an educational setting

- Defining, describing or presenting the facts on a topic

- Helping people understand something complex or foreign to them

A particular kind of informative speech is sometimes called the "demonstrative speech" or the "how-to" presentation. This is where you show or demonstrate how something is done, such as how to draw a cartoon bear or how to buy a used car.

By definition an informative speech presents the facts or information the audience will need, and it avoids the opinions or conclusions of the speaker. The format (organization) of the talk may simply consist of covering a handful of topics in a particular order. Depending on the topic, however, the talk may be better organized as a sequence of logic, changes, actions, etc.

PERSUASIVE

If you are trying to persuade someone of something, you could call it a "persuasive speech." Here are some examples:

- Trying to get people to buy something or support a cause

- Trying to change people's feelings, ideas or opinions about a person or thing

- Making an important proposal in the form of a presentation to a group

A particular kind of persuasive speech could be considered the "motivational speech" or the "call-to-action speech." Here the speaker is not only trying to persuade, but to also have such a strong emotional impact that people in the audience will want to go into action—to *do something about it*.

Persuasive talks often work best with an overall thesis-type organization, where the thesis is clearly stated, the arguments for and against are logically laid out, and the conclusion is a restatement of the thesis. Whereas the informative speech is inclined to let the audience make its own conclusions or decisions about the information, in a persuasive speech there is a conclusion or decision the speaker is trying to bring the audience to agree with or support.

SPECIAL OCCASION

This is a sort of catch-all category for other types of speeches. Here are some examples:

- Ceremonies, such as weddings, funerals, graduations, awards events, etc.

- Entertainment, such as "after-dinner" talks, roasts, celebrations, etc.

- Introductions, toasts, congratulations, welcomes

Clearly, special occasion speeches vary widely depending on the activity and purpose of the speech.

COMBINATIONS

Many speeches will combine these types. For example, a persuasive speech might include information to support the main argument, making part of the talk look like an "informative speech." Meanwhile, an informative speech might include an introduction to someone else or a humorous story, making part of the speech look like a "special occasion speech." The type of speech, or combination of types, is usually not important. What's important is that you are successful in getting your ideas across effectively and creating the effect you want to create on your audience.

4

Speech Writing Basics

Speech Writing Basics

4

There are essentially three steps to a good speech:

A. It's well written

B. It's well rehearsed

C. It's well delivered

For an effective five-minute speech, one might spend many hours on A, an hour or so on B and five minutes (it's a five-minute speech) on C. That's right—though it might seem odd at first, a truly effective short speech will usually require more time to prepare than a longer, less formal speech.

However that may or may not prove true for you, it is safe to say that your audiences will appreciate every hour you spend editing to make your presentations both better *and* shorter.

In this light, let's consider some speech writing basics.

• Know your audience.

You need to understand who you are talking to, as it will affect countless decisions you make while writing your talk. What vocabulary do they understand? What do they care about? What might they find offensive or strongly disagreeable? What might need more explanation? How much time are they expecting the talk to take? What are they expecting to get out of the talk? And so on.

You can write a great talk—but if it's for the wrong audience, it will fail.

- Have something to say that is worth saying—a clear, useful message.

A message is anything a writer or speaker wants to get across. The key is knowing what that message is and why it's important to the audience before constructing the talk. If the message is not clear and truly worth sharing to you, it has no chance of being clear and useful to the audience.

Part of this concerns your actual ownership of the message. Novice writers and speakers often give a summary of other people's information and ideas and leave it at that. Unfortunately, such an approach will normally result in a less-than-successful talk. The audience wants to hear what *the speaker* thinks or has to say. The message may include data from someone else or even someone else's point of view, but speakers should still *own* the data and have a message of their own—as appropriate to the setting.

- Support your opinions, general statements, evaluations and conclusions with specific details and facts.

You have to say enough to make your points realistic to your audience. Saying enough, however, doesn't necessarily mean using a lot of words. It means giving enough details and specifics to help the audience "see" what you're trying to say.

This is also where an anecdote or story can be useful—never to substitute for hard facts, but to help ground your message or an important point you are trying to make.

- Write a talk, not an essay.

As opposed to a piece of writing, in a speech you can use visual or audiovisual aids, you can ask the audience questions, you can pause for several seconds in the middle of your talk, you can pass things out for a demonstration, you can have audience members come up—in short, there are things you can do in a live presentation that you just can't do in an essay, things that will help you engage your audience and communicate more effectively.

So, though you may be writing and editing your talk just as you might an essay or other piece of writing, remember that it isn't a piece of writing but a talk. If you've ever heard someone give a speech by basically just reading an essay they've written, you'll understand this point. You're going to give a talk, so be sure to write a talk.

- Trim, refine, edit.

The best speeches are always well edited and trim. They don't waste words. They don't waste time. They leave the audience interested and wanting more.

SUMMARY

- Know your audience. Write a talk for them, not someone else.

- Have something worthwhile to say—a message that is *yours*.

- Give enough details to back up your points and keep it interesting.

- Write a talk, not an essay. Make it live and engaging.

- Trim, refine, edit. Make the talk efficient.

If you do these things in writing a speech, and then spend adequate time practicing, you have a very good chance of success when it comes time to deliver the speech to an audience.

5

Speech Delivery Basics

Speech Delivery Basics

You've prepared an excellent speech that you are sure will communicate effectively to your audience. Now it's time to actually *deliver* it.

So, how exactly is that done?

There are many answers to that question, and you have already done much to answer the question for yourself. But let's look more closely at this by taking up three essential basics.

MANNERS

Though the finer details of etiquette vary from place to place and can change over time, basic good manners never go out of style. Using common sense and good manners in any public speaking situation is a basic that should never be overlooked.

Some simple points include dressing appropriately, being respectful of your audience, being well-prepared, facing and looking at your audience, being willing and interested in hearing audience questions or thoughts, and so on.

Knowing expected points of etiquette is always wise. But more fundamentally, you will almost always win if you apply the Golden Rule by treating the audience as you would want to be treated.

You may have a great talk, but one major manners faux pas (false step) can send your talk irrecoverably off the cliff.

NOTES AND OTHER AIDS

In some form or another, notes can be used to help you get through a talk successfully without getting lost or omitting something important. Yes, it is sometimes possible and even necessary to deliver a speech with no notes at all, but we'll take that up later. For now, let's consider several basic public speaking aids, including notes.

1. Outlines

   Most speeches are based on outlines. In fact, many talks are never fully written out but are simply outlined. Even a fully written talk is often translated into an outline form for the purpose of delivery. This is different than the outline used to organize the writing of a paper or speech. This is an outline specifically to organize the talk and, as such, can take any form useful to the speaker.

   A common method of preparing for a talk is to practice giving the talk word-for-word, but with an eye on the overall outline or structure. Gradually, you acquire a good feel for the talk and know the overall outline either mentally or with brief reference to notes. You know you won't get lost. The talk itself isn't given word-for-word, but close enough to serve. You've practiced it enough that all you need is the overall outline.

2. Notecards

   People often put little pieces of a speech onto small notecards they can hold and refer to while giving a talk. What you put on the notecards can be key reminder words or phrases, or even whole sentences or paragraphs that you need or want to ensure you say exactly word for word (such as a quote from a named source).

   An advantage to notecards is they can fit in a pocket and are small enough to hold in your hand. You don't need to have a podium on which to set them down, for example, which gives you the freedom to move around. Even if you have a clicker in your hand to control images on a screen behind or beside you, you can still hold and move through notecards fairly easily.

3. Written Speech

In less formal talks, a speaker may choose to bring his full speech printed out. A large font will make it easy to read, though it will add to the number of pages. To avoid just reading the talk and not addressing the audience well, speakers will highlight key words or passages they can quickly glance at to keep themselves on track.

The advantage to this is that anything you want to ensure gets said exactly, whether it's an important point, a very specific argument, a quote, a group of statistics, etc., you can feel confident of getting right without having to memorize it. And having the whole talk in front of you makes it harder (though not impossible) to get lost.

4. Teleprompters

A teleprompter is a device that allows the speaker to look directly into a video camera and read text projected on a mirror in front of the camera lens. The speaker (actor, news reporter, etc.) looks directly into the camera, reading the text of his speech, lines, report, etc. Another type of teleprompter consists of a pair of glass panes on stands, placed at a distance in front to the right and left of a podium. The speaker can see the words as they scroll forward, while the audience cannot.

Someone experienced in the use of a teleprompter (or "prompter") can look quite natural and be very effective as a public speaker. As they look at the audience, shifting their glance from left to right (in the case of the latter type), they can pick up the words on the prompters and maintain good communication. As with any other aid, teleprompters can help, but they can't make a good public speaker out of a bad one.

5. Presentation Software

There are a number of well-known programs for use in designing visual presentations. These programs can be invaluable in providing graphic representations, animations, charts and a wide variety of other visual aids.

As the speaker, you can also use presentations prepared in this way as a sort of outline or notes for yourself. As you move through the presentation slides, you are able to follow along with your talk exactly as you created it with the presentation software. In this way, you may not need other notes.

A word of warning—it takes a bit of skill to use presentation software well. Potential errors are limitless, but include these:

- Showing a 3-minute video as part of a 5-minute talk where the video is not the main point of the presentation

- Too much text on slides

- Text not everyone can easily read

- Silly graphics or "catchy" animations that don't enhance the message but instead make a talk appear amateurish

NO NOTES AT ALL

Some talks are prepared that are twenty or more minutes in length and the speaker uses no notes of any kind, nor teleprompter, notecards or presentation software.

One category of these "no-notes" public speakers are more properly thought of as performers. Actors on the stage, singers and magicians perform without notes, though they all have props, cues or things they can use as reminders for what's next. It's possible that stand-up comics have the toughest job of all these types of performers, for they usually have no props and must not only remember many jokes told in a specific way with specific timing but transitions between sets of jokes as well.

Sticking with what we think of as public speaking more strictly, there can be situations where a lengthy talk must essentially be learned completely and the notes or aids will be few or none at all. In such a case, any of the aids can prove useful in the learning stage, but ultimately there will be no substitute for extensive practice. Individuals have been known to practice for weeks to give a single successful twenty-minute presentation, particularly when the person, though intelligent and successful, isn't an experienced public speaker. Who knows but that may someday be you!

PRACTICE

Finally, there is simply no substitute for practice.

If you've prepared an excellent speech, the best way to ensure your delivery is excellent will be practice. And it is recommended that you practice with a test audience of one or more persons you can trust to give you useful feedback on what is working and what isn't.

SUMMARY

Here then, in summary, are some simple speech delivery basics:

1. Use good manners to ensure smooth interaction with your audience.

2. Use outlines or notes as appropriate or needed.

3. If possible, use presentation software (audio-visual aids) to enhance your message.

4. Practice, practice, practice.

6

Opening and Closing
a Speech

Opening and Closing a Speech 6

OPENINGS

There are many ways a speech, talk or presentation can be started. What follows are a handful of ideas. Many other ideas exist or could be created.

1. A simple statement of the topic

    Today I'd like to talk to you about why you'll be glad your car will soon be driving itself. That's right: you will be glad your car drives itself!

2. A reference to the occasion

    What an honor to be celebrating the company's 25th anniversary with all of you!

3. A personal greeting or reference

    It's great to be back with all my school friends and faculty, so many of whom helped launch me on my entrepreneurial career.

4. A question to get the audience thinking

    When was the last time you helped a stranger?

5. An alarming or enlightening fact

    The average U.S. child spends over 5 hours watching TV, movies or playing video games for every hour reading for pleasure.

6. A quotation

The famous 20ᵗʰ century painter Henri Matisse once said, "Creativity takes courage."

7. An anecdote

My grandmother died at 96. Though she only finished sixth grade, when I was a high school senior and she was in her eighties, I remember that her handwriting was beautiful, her spelling perfect, and her arithmetic quick. Her six years of schooling embarrassed my twelve.

8. The thesis statement for a persuasive speech

We could learn so much from the legalization of marijuana in several U.S. states, but unless it is declassified as a federally controlled substance, we won't. Why? Because vendors are, in effect, having to run a semi-legal business and free market rules therefore do not apply.

If you look over each of the above openings one more time, you will notice whether or not they attract your attention and prepare you very briefly for what will follow. And that could be said to define the purpose for an opening—*to attract attention and orient the audience to where you intend to take them.*

Strong speech openings are often memorized.

CLOSINGS

The following are some ideas for closings. Again, many other ideas for closings exist or could be created.

Note that the closing can be influenced by the opening if for no other reason than it is natural to come back around to the main message, thesis, question or theme you began with. For this reason, you will find the following closing ideas similar to the openings covered earlier.

1. A simple re-statement of the topic or primary message

   So if you're anything like me, you can't wait until your car finally takes over all the mindless work of getting us from here to there every day—and you get all that productive time back!

2. A statement for the future

   Let's decide today that the next 25 years will be even more rewarding than the first 25 have been!

3. A validation of the audience

   Without all the support and encouragement—and ruthless competition—so many of you provided me, I would never have found the endless challenge and joy available to those of us who make their lives all about starting businesses from scratch and watching them grow on their own. So, thank you all.

4. An answer to (or restatement of) a question

   In my case, I can now say, every day, the last time I helped a stranger was today. or *So, I leave you with the question I opened with: When was the last time you helped a stranger?*

5. A solution, conclusion or assertion

   My contention is simple and it's this: Implementation of these simple guidelines in our own homes virtually guarantees our children will grow up better readers—AND better programmers—than we are.

6. A quotation

   As I began with a quotation, let me end with one: "Freedom lies in being bold." Robert Frost.

7. An anecdote

   My grandmother never enlightened me on sociology, trigonometry or marine biology—but I never met her peer for beautiful handwriting, perfect spelling or quick arithmetic.

8. The thesis statement for a persuasive speech

   Until it is declassified as a federally controlled substance, we'll never know what effects the free market might have on the sale, distribution and popular use of marijuana.

A good closing will wrap up the topic for the listener, summarizing important points or the overall message, or otherwise arriving at the overall purpose of the talk. It will smoothly bring the talk to a close. As with a strong opening, a strong closing is often memorized, even when the rest of the talk is only done from a general outline.

7

Common Public Speaking Errors

Common Public Speaking Errors

Those who give public presentations should be aware of some common errors which can greatly reduce their effectiveness as speakers.

1. Not being well-enough prepared

    Being well prepared can cover many things: the physical space and equipment; any digital information, including charts, diagrams, facts and figures; knowing what questions might come up; being well rehearsed; and so on. Perhaps there's nothing worse than being in the middle of a presentation and finding out you are insufficiently prepared. Imagine you are a lawyer with a case to plead! Do your homework and don't get caught missing key data.

2. Acting nervous, rushing

    Inexperienced performers often rush because they get nervous and adrenaline kicks in. This is true of amateur musicians, actors, and even athletes in critical situations. For a public speaker, it can mean talking so fast that words aren't understandable. Or it can just mean the presentation feels rushed and not relaxed. If you feel nervous, make an effort to slow down, smile, and do everything you can to look relaxed, even if you don't feel it. Experience will teach you that no matter how nervous you feel, if you look and act relaxed, 99% of the time the audience will be focused on your presentation and your message, not on you and your nerves. Professionals are not always relaxed but they always *look* relaxed—and they don't rush.

3. Mispronouncing words or names

    This is most common in students who are researching areas they have never talked to anyone about. Especially when preparing a presentation, discipline yourself to clear up the pronunciation of a word you don't know how to say. Saying the word incorrectly can cause you to be misunderstood, or make you look ignorant—or both. Mispronouncing names can be even worse. In addition to the above-mentioned problems, a mispronounced name can offend others, especially if it is the name of someone present or someone or someplace the audience has a connection to.

4. Subconsciously using filler words or other mannerisms

    A mannerism such as fiddling with your glasses or a filler word such as "um" or "you know" may go unnoticed in casual conversation. Yet in public speaking situations, when one is likely more nervous, it can become exaggerated and be very distracting to the audience. Some common filler words include these:

    - *so* as an opening to talks, paragraphs and sentences
    - *basically* as a useless insert when one is indefinite
    - *uh, um* as a sign of uncertainty or discomfort when pausing
    - *like* as a meaningless filler
    - *right?* as a repeated request for affirmation

    You should watch for filler words and nervous mannerisms in your public speaking and do whatever you can to eliminate them.

5. Failing to follow a sound line of reasoning

    Using sound reasoning in preparing and giving a presentation is possibly so fundamental that people overlook its importance. Comb through your presentation carefully, looking for points of illogic that might cause your audience to lose you. Be sure to look *from the audience's point of view*—what may seem perfectly logical to you may not make sense to your audience.

Note especially any places you had to convince yourself it made sense; others will probably have the same problem.

6. Not having or emphasizing a single, clear-cut point

    Having a clear intention of what you are trying to get across is again so basic it can be missed. The simpler and more clear-cut you can make your message—even if it is simply to fully inform your audience on a given topic—the greater your odds are for success. You'd be surprised how many talks fail mainly because there wasn't any single, simple, clear idea being communicated.

7. Failing to provide specifics

    If you are trying to persuade, you will need good specifics. If you are trying to entertain, you will need good specifics. If you are trying to inform, you will need good specifics. In short, good talks have good specifics and lack of them is a common error.

Having discussed common errors, it's worth keeping in mind that the senior purpose of any public talk is to communicate effectively. The errors are mentioned only because they can get in the way of effective communication. It's possible that a *great* speech could contain every one of the above errors, but the communication of the speech was so strong and so powerful that the errors couldn't block or inhibit the message and its effectiveness.

Eliminate errors for better communication. But whatever you do, don't stop communicating. That would be the biggest error of all!